All About Nature

Animals, Insects, Plants, and More!

words by
Huda Harajl

pictures by
Jane Sanders

callisto
publishing
an imprint of Sourcebooks

Copyright © 2024 by Callisto Publishing LLC
Cover and internal design © 2024 by Callisto Publishing LLC
Illustrations by Jane Sanders
Series Designer: Liz Cosgrove
Art Director: Angela Navarra
Art Producer: Stacey Stambaugh
Editor: Mo Mozuch
Production Editor: Rachel Taenzler
Production Manager: Martin Worthington

Published by Callisto Publishing LLC C/O Sourcebooks LLC
P.O. Box 4410, Naperville, Illinois 60567-4410
(630) 961-3900
callistopublishing.com

Printed and bound in Canada.
Friesens 10 9 8 7 6 5 4 3 2 1

For Hassan and Emily: May you forever find wonder and peace in the beauty of nature.

What is nature? Grab your shoes and magnifying glass. Step outside to find out!

Look at the tree, and feel the warm sunshine.
Smell the flowers, and hear the birds chirping.
Nature is all around us!

Nature is the ground we walk on.
It is the wind, water, sky, and **sun**.
It is the plants and **animals**.
It is not cars or houses.

Nature is everything in our world not made by people.

We live on planet **Earth**. Earth is shaped like a ball. It is made up of rocks, water, and air.

Look up! What is happening in the sky? As the Earth spins around the sun, the light and weather changes.

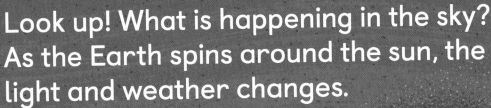

The sun is the closest star to Earth. It provides light and warmth to people, plants, and animals.

The sun is a huge star! One million Earths could fit inside the sun.

As the Earth spins, sunlight reaches half of the Earth. Daytime is when you are in the half that is light.

Look, it's daytime! During the **day**, you can ride your bike in the park. You can play outside and go on picnics.

You can see your shadow during the day.

As the Earth spins, one side turns away
from the sun. The sky becomes dark. The
air feels cooler. This is nighttime.

What do you see in the **night** sky? You can see the moon and stars. You can see the moon because it reflects light from the sun.

Did you know the moon is over four billion years old?

You can count stars in the night sky.
Camping at night is also fun.

You might hear an owl during the night.
"Hoo! Hoo!" What else do you hear?

Look out the window.
What do you see?
The sky!

On a clear day, the sky is blue. When the **weather** changes, the sky can look gray, cloudy, or rainy.

What is weather? Weather is what we see and feel outside. Weather can be rainy, cloudy, windy, stormy, snowy, or sunny.

Weather is a part of nature.
How do you decide what to wear outside?
The weather!

Fog is a cloud that is on the ground.

Weather changes as **seasons** change.
Many places on Earth have four seasons.

The four seasons are spring, summer, fall, and winter. What is your favorite season?

Splash! Water is everywhere. All living things need water. It is an important part of nature.

Water covers most of Earth. **Oceans** are large bodies of water.

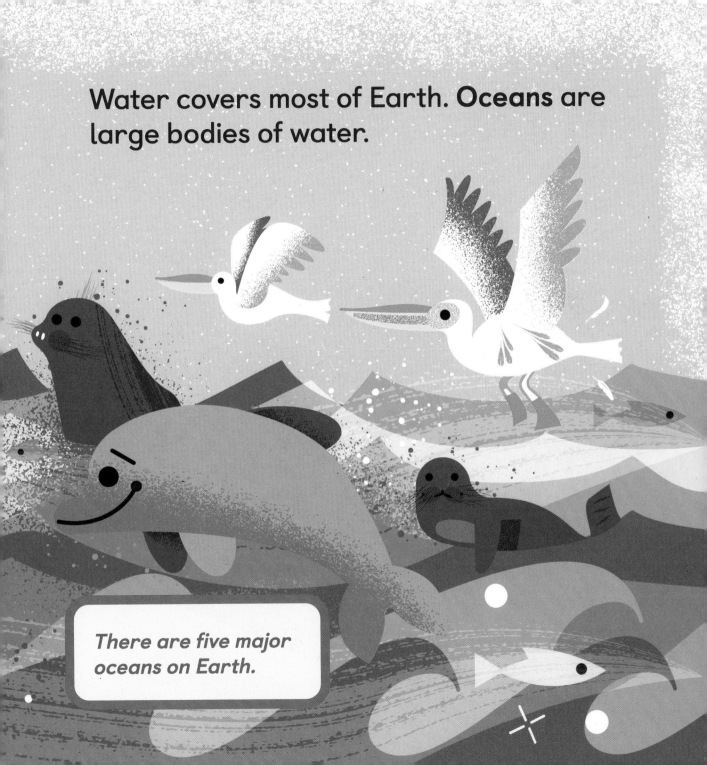

There are five major oceans on Earth.

Water is also in **lakes** and **rivers**. Ducks, fish, turtles, and otters live in rivers.

Water is all around us. You can build sandcastles at the beach. You can dip your toes in the cold water.

Look down! What is that under your feet? It is the ground.

Subsoil

Topsoil

Substratum

Bedrock

The ground is made up of **soil** and **rocks**. Below it are more rocks and dirt that we cannot see.

Watertable

Can you find a rock? Is it bumpy or smooth? What color is your rock? Does it sparkle?

Rocks are made up of **minerals**.
There are many different types of rocks.
How many can you find?

CHALK

GRANITE

SHALE

SANDSTONE

CLAY

Rocks are used to make buildings, roads, jewelry, and more.

Smell the flowers, look up at the tall trees, and feel the grass under your feet. Plants are everywhere!

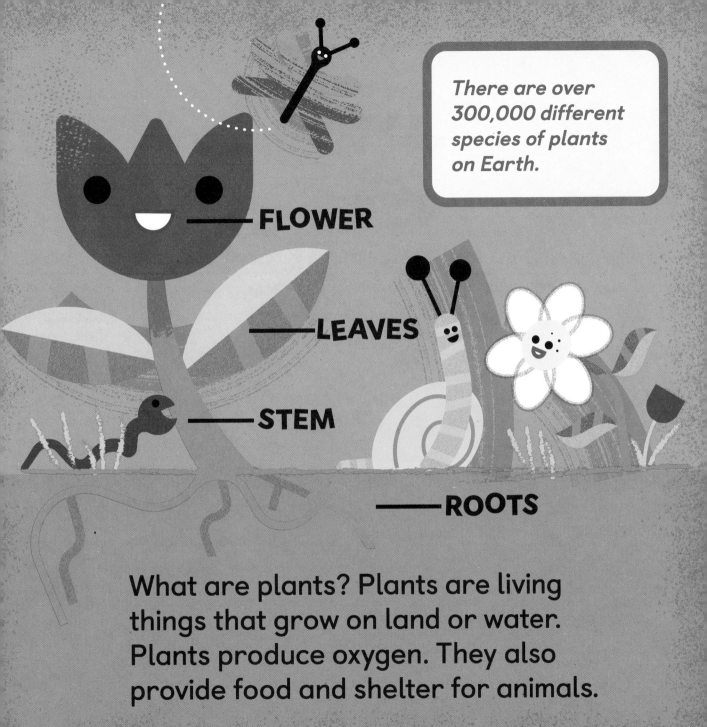

FLOWER

LEAVES

STEM

ROOTS

There are over 300,000 different species of plants on Earth.

What are plants? Plants are living things that grow on land or water. Plants produce oxygen. They also provide food and shelter for animals.

Trees, bushes, flowers, and grass are some plants you might see every day.

Many of the foods we eat come from plants. Apples, bananas, carrots, and pumpkins all come from plants.

Can you find the dog, bird, and cat? They are all animals. But what is an animal?

Some animals, like chameleons and octopuses, can change colors!

An animal is a living thing. Animals come in many different shapes and sizes. They can have fur or feathers. Some even have scales.

Animals are all around us. They live in nature and in our homes and backyards. Some animals live in the water, and others live on land. Animals live on every corner of the earth.

All animals need food and water to live.
They can move around, eat, breathe,
and grow.

Buzz! It is a bee! A bee is a type of insect.

Ant

Bee

Insects come in different shapes.
Some are colorful, like ladybugs and
butterflies.

Other bugs, like ants and bees, might bite or sting. What is your favorite kind of bug?

Butterfly

Ladybug

All insects have three body segments and six legs.

People are living things just like plants, animals, and bugs. We need air to breathe, water to drink, and food to eat.

We are all part of nature and must take care of it. We should keep the air and water clean. It is important to be gentle with all living things.

Now you are an expert on nature!
What is your favorite part of nature?

Glossary

animals: living creatures that can move around, eat, breathe, and grow

day: when the sky is bright because you're in the sunny half of Earth.

Earth: the planet we live on, covered in land, water, and air

insect: small animal with three body parts and six legs

lake: a body of water surrounded by land on all sides

minerals: solid materials found in nature, such as gold

nature: everything around us that is not made by people, like trees, plants, rocks, and animals

night: when the sky is dark because you're not in the sunny half of Earth.

ocean: the largest body of water on Earth

river: a stream of water that flows into the ocean

rocks: hard, solid things like stones and pebbles found in nature

seasons: different times of the year when weather changes: fall, winter, spring, and summer

soil: natural material that covers the ground and helps plants grow

sun: a star that gives off light and heat and is the center of our solar system

weather: the way the air and sky feel outside, like sunny, stormy, cloudy, windy, rainy, or snowy

About the Author

 **Huda Harajli** is an author and educator based in Michigan. She holds both graduate and undergraduate degrees from the University of Michigan, where she honed her passion for education and literature. She loves the four seasons that Michigan offers and she enjoys spending time outdoors with her husband and daughter.

About the Illustrator

Jane Sanders illustrates children's books, magazines, newspapers, and even toy packaging. When Jane is not drawing, she loves to walk her poodle and French bulldog.